Emerald Law

The English Legal System

Anthony Chadwick

Emerald Publishing

British Cataloguing in Publication data. A catalogue record is
available for this book from the British Library.

ISBN 1903909 92 9

Printed in the United Kingdom by Webspeed Books Beds
www.webspeedbooks.com

Cover Design by Bookworks Islington

Contents

Introduction

7 Civil Cases 75

Index

Introduction

This first edition of Emerald law-Guide to the English Legal System is wide ranging and covers all the main areas of our complex legal system in depth.

For the average person, the legal system in this country can appear mystifying. All they know is that the process of funding legal cases costs a lot of money. However, for most of us in our lives, one way or another, we will find ourselves in court.

It is very important for a citizen to have a clear idea of how the legal system operates and who is who in the system, the role of the judiciary, the European Courts and also the availability of funding if a case needs to go to court and is proving to expensive.

One of the main axioms of the last ten years or so has been access to justice. How easily can individuals and others access the legal system in this country. It is true that the system has become more accessible and easier to understand. However, that doesn't take away the fact that the process is daunting.

This introduction to the English legal System should prove invaluable to all, student, professional and layperson.

Anthony Chadwick

1

The Framework of Law

Law covers a wide variety of areas. There are different categories of law: national law; international law which is divided into public and private law and further sub-categories discussed later.

International law

International law concerns itself with inter-nation disputes and conflict. This law, in the main, derives from various treaties which have been agreed over time between different governments.

National law

This is the law which applies within each individual nation. Within national law there is a distinction between public and private law. Public law involves the government or state in some way and private law is concerned with disputes and conflict between individuals and businesses. Public and private law, as mentioned can be further sub-divided.

Public law

There are three distinct areas of public law:

1. Constitutional law

Constitutional law controls and sets out the framework for government, and methods of government.

2. Administrative law

This controls how the ministers of government, both national and local, can operate. A key part of administrative law is that of the right to judicial review of decisions made by government.

3. Criminal law

Criminal law deals with the types of behaviour, whether individual or on a business level, which are considered outside the boundaries of the general law and accepted moral codes and which are punishable. A person who commits a crime is said to have offended against the State and the State has the right to prosecute them and punish them if found guilty.

Private law

Private law is usually termed civil law and there are many differing branches. The main ones dealing with everyday matters are family law, contract law, tort (negligence) company law and employment law.

Civil law is very different in nature from criminal law. Whereas criminal law deals with crimes against the state private or civil law deals with disputes between individuals

Distinctions between criminal law cases and civil cases

There are key differences between criminal and civil cases. The cases take place in different courts. In general, criminal law cases will be heard in either Magistrates Courts or the Crown Court. Civil cases are heard either in the High Court or, more often than not, in the County Court. Some civil cases, especially matters concerning family, can be heard in the Magistrates Court.

In criminal cases, the terminology used to describe key personnel is different to that of those involved in civil cases. The person commencing a criminal case is called a prosecutor, whilst in civil cases they are called the claimant.

In criminal cases, the terminology used generally is different. A person is either found guilty or not guilty. In a civil case a defendant is found liable or not liable. At the end of a criminal case, the person, if found guilty, will be punished and sentenced appropriately. In a civil case, the person if found to be liable will be ordered to put right the matter. This is usually done by an award of money as compensation, known as damages although other remedies may be ordered.

In criminal cases, the standard of proof is very high. A criminal case must be proven beyond all reasonable doubt. Civil cases are proved on the balance of probabilities. This is a lower standard of proof.

Below is a summary of civil and criminal law cases.

	Civil cases	Criminal cases
Object of law	To uphold the rights of individuals	To maintain law and order
Person starting case	Individuals who are affected	Usually State through police or Crown Prosecution Service
Terminology	Claimant	Prosecutor
Courts	County Court or High Court or Tribunal	Magistrates court or Crown Court
Standard of proof	The balance of probability	Beyond reasonable doubt
People making Decision	Judge	Magistrates or jury
Decision	Liable or not liable	Guilty or not guilty
Powers of court	Usually damages, injunction, performance of contract rescission or rectification	Prison, fine, community order, discharge etc.

Defining law

Having considered the various divisions of law it is now time to consider definitions of law. One broad definition of law was that provided by Sir John Salmond. He defined the law as being 'the body of principles recognised and applied by the state in the administration of justice'. This neatly encapsulates the meaning and application of law in one brief sentence.

Law applies throughout a country to people generally. There are other sets of rules applied more individually to people and organisations, for example rules governing sports or rules which have developed as a result of local customs and traditions.

Law and morality

Moral values of communities set out a framework for how people should behave. Concepts of morality differ from culture to culture, although there are common denominators, for example outlawing extreme and harmful behaviour such as rape or murder. Morality often springs from a religious base, the bible for Christians and the Koran for Muslims are key examples. The law of a country will, usually, reflect the moral values accepted by most of a country but will differ in certain aspects. One example is that adultery is often considered a crime in Muslim countries but not so in Christian countries.

In England and Wales there has been a move away from religious belief and the development of law reflects this. For example a limited form of euthanasia has been accepted as legal, as reflected in the ruling in Airedale NHS Trust v Bland (1993), where it was ruled that medical staff could withdraw life support systems from a patient who could breathe unaided but who was in a persistent vegetative state. Similarly, with abortion which is legalised. Whilst there are many groups who believe that euthanasia and abortion are immoral the law has moved differently.

Law and justice

Although justice is the main goal of the law it doesn't always provide a just outcome. There is the problem of defining justice as was outlined by Lord Wright, who said:

' *the guiding principle of a judge in deciding cases is to do justice; that is justice according to the law, but still justice. I have not found any satisfactory definition of justice…what is just in a particular case is what appears just to the just man, in the same way as what is reasonable appears to be reasonable to the reasonable man'.*

In many circumstances people's concepts of justice will be different. For example, the situation where a person uses force to repel a burglar and injures that person. This has been the cause of many a heated debate, from one end of the spectrum where it is thought right to be able to defend and kill in the process to the other end where it is seen as only right to defend but not injure. No doubt this debate will rage on forever more. This example highlights differing views on concepts of justice.

Rights and duties of individuals under the law

The law gives rights to individuals. It also gives methods of enforcing those rights if violated. The law also imposes duties on individuals. Rights and duties run through many areas such as contract and employment and also runs through criminal law, imposing a duty on the individual to obey the law and a right of the state to punish.

2

Development of law

The law in England and Wales has developed gradually over time. Law has been developed in a number of different ways, and the methods of developing law are known as sources of law. Historically, the most important ways were custom and decisions of judges. Parliament became more powerful in the eighteenth and nineteenth centuries, with Acts of Parliament becoming the main source of new laws, although judicial decisions were, and are, still important. During the twentieth century, statute law and judicial decisions continued to be the main sources of law, but increasingly two new sources of law became important: delegated legislation and European legislation. Together, all these sources of law have combined to create the present day legal system.

Customs

Customs are rules of behaviour which develop in a community. There are two main types of custom: general and local customs.

General customs

General customs are common customs which have developed and have been absorbed over time into law.

Local customs

Local customs is a term used where a person claims that he or she is entitled to some local right, such as a right of way or the right to use land in a certain way, because this is what has happened locally over time. Judge have a test of what constitutes local customs. These are as follows:

- The custom must have existed since 'time immemorial
- The custom must have been exercised peaceably openly and as of right
- The custom must be definite as to locality, nature and scope
- The custom must be reasonable

It is very rare for a new custom to be considered by courts nowadays. There have been certain exceptions. For example, in Egerton v Harding (1974) the court decided that there was a customary duty to fence land against cattle straying from the common. Although customs develop they are not part of the law until recognised by the courts.

Common law

The legal system historically could not rely on customs alone. In Anglo-Saxon times there were local courts that decided disputes but it was not until after the Norman conquest in 1066 that a more organised system of courts developed. Norman kings realised that control of the country was that much easier if the legal system was also controlled. William the Conqueror set up the Curia Regis

(The Kings Court) and appointed judges to hear disputes from the nobles. In addition to this central court, judges were sent to major towns to decide important cases.

In the time of Henry 11 (1154-89) these tours became more regular and the country was divided up into circuits, or areas for the judges to visit. Initially the judges would use the local customs or the old Anglo-Saxon laws to decide cases. On return to London the judges would discuss customs and gradually these evolved into a uniform or common law.

Common law is the basis of our law today, an unwritten law that developed from customs and judicial decisions. The phrase 'common law' is still used to distinguish laws that have been developed by judicial decisions, from laws that have been created by statute or other legislation. For example murder is a common law crime whilst theft is a statutory crime.

Common law also has another meaning. It is used to distinguish between rules that were developed by the common law courts (the Kings Courts) and the rules of equity which were developed by the Lord Chancellor and the Chancery Courts.

Equity

Historically this is an important source still playing a part today with many of our legal concepts having developed from equitable principles. The word 'equity' has a meaning of fairness and this is the basis on which it operates.

Equity developed because of problems in the common law. Only certain types of cases were recognised. The law was also very technical; if there was an error in the formalities the person making the claim would lose the case. People who could not obtain justice in the common law courts appealed to the King. Most of these cases were referred to the Kings Chancellor. This was because the Chancellor based his decisions on principles of natural justice and fairness, making a decision on what seemed right in a particular case as opposed to the strict following of previous precedents. Account was also taken of what the parties had originally intended.

To ensure that decisions were fair, new procedures were introduced such as subpoenas, which ordered a witness to attend court. New remedies for compensation were developed which were able to compensate plaintiffs more fully than those previously used. The main equitable remedies were: injunctions; specific performance; rescission and rectification. These are all still in use today and will be explained more fully later on in this book.

Judicial precedents

The doctrine of precedents

Judicial precedent refers to the source of law where decisions of judges in the past create law for future judges to follow. This source of law is also known as case law and is a major source of law.

The English system of precedent is based on the Latin maxim *stare decisis et non quieta movere* Whish is usually shortened to *stare decisis* and which translated means 'stand by what has been decided and do not unsettle the established'. This supports the idea of fairness and certainty in law.

Ratio Decidendi

Precedent is only relevant and can only be effective if the reasons for past decisions are known. Judges will outline reasons for decisions and the rationale for a judgement outlining the principles of law used. These principles are an important part of any judgement and are known as the *ratio decidendi* which means the reason for deciding. This is what creates the precedent for future judges to follow.

Obiter Dicta

The remainder of the judgement is called *obiter dicta* (other things said) and judges in future cases do not have to follow it.

Original precedent

If the point of law in a case has never been decided before, then whatever the judge decides will form a new precedent for future cases to follow. As there are no past cases for a judge to base his decision on, he is likely to look at cases which are the closest in principle and he may decide to use similar rules. This way of arriving at a judgement is called reasoning by analogy. The idea of creating new law by analogy can be seen in Hunter and others v Canary Wharf Limited and London Docklands Development Corporation (1995). Part of the decision involved whether the interference with television reception was capable of constituting an actionable private nuisance. The facts of the case were that the main tower Canary Wharf built in the Isle of Dogs East London, was 250 metres high and 50 metres square. The claimant and others claimed damages from the defendant for continuing interference over a number of years with the television reception in the area as a result of the height of the tower.

In the Court of Appeal, the Lord Justice Pill stated:

'Lord Irving (counsel for the defendants) submits that interference with television reception by reason of the presence of a building is properly to be regarded as analogous to loss of aspect (view). To obstruct the receipt of television signals by the erection of a building between the point of receipt and the source is not in law a nuisance............... I accept the importance of television in the lives of people. However, in my judgement the erection or presence of a building in the line of sight between a television transmitter and other properties is not actionable as an interference with the use and enjoyment of land. The analogy with loss of prospect is compelling. The loss of a view, which may be of the greatest importance to householders, is not actionable and neither is the mere presence of a building in the site lines to the television transmitter'.

Binding precedent

This is a precedent from an earlier case which must be followed even if the judge in the later case does not agree with the principle. A binding precedent is only created where the facts of the second case are sufficiently similar to the original case.

Persuasive precedent

This is a precedent that is not binding on the court but the judge may consider it and decide that it is a correct principle and is persuaded that it should be followed. Persuasive precedent comes from a number of sources:

- Courts lower in the hierarchy
- Decisions by the Judicial Committee of the Privy Council
- Statements made obiter dicta
- A dissenting judgement
- Decisions of courts in foreign countries.

The hierarchy of courts and precedent

In England and Wales courts operate a rigid hierarchy of judicial precedents. Every court is bound to follow any decision made by a court above it in the hierarchy. In general appellate courts (appeal courts) are bound by their own decisions.

The diagram overleaf indicates the hierarchy of courts.

Civil cases

Criminal cases

European Court of Justice
Justice

European Court of
Justice

|

|

House of Lords

House of Lords

|

|

Court of Appeal
(Civil Division)

Court of Appeal
(Criminal Division)

|

|

Divisional Courts

Queens Bench Divisional
Court

|

|

High Court

Crown Court

|

|

County Court

Magistrates Court

|

Magistrates Court

The European Court of Justice

The highest court affecting the legal system in England and Wales is the European Court of Justice. This has been the case since 1973. For points of European law, a decision made by this court is binding on all other courts in England and Wales. There are still laws unaffected by European Union law and for these the House of Lords is the supreme court.

House of Lords

The House of Lords is the most senior court nationally and its decisions bind all other courts in the English legal system. The House of Lords is not bound by its past decisions, even though it will generally follow them.

The main debate about the House of Lords is the extent to which it should follow its own decisions and the ideas regarding this have changed over the years. Originally, the view was that the House of Lords had the right to overrule its own past decisions but this has changed. In one seminal case, *London Street Tramways v London County Council (1898)* The house of Lords held that certainty in the law was more important than the possibility of hardship being caused by the need to follow past decisions. From 1898 to 1966 the House of Lords regarded itself as being completely bound by its own past decisions unless that decision was made in error *(per incuriam)*. However, this idea of error referred only to situations where a decision had been made without considering the effect of a relevant statute.

This was felt to be unsatisfactory as the law could not alter to meet changing social conditions and opinions nor could any 'wrong decisions' be changed by the courts. If there was an unsatisfactory decision made by the House of Lords then the only way to change it was by passing an Act of Parliament.

It was realised that the House of Lords should have more flexibility and, in 1966, the Lord Chancellor issued a Practice Statement announcing a change to the rule in London Street Tramways v London County Council, which said as follows:

' *Their Lordships regard the use of precedent as an indispensable foundation upon which to decide what is the law and its application in individual cases. It provides at least some degree of certainty upon which individuals can rely in the conduct of their own affairs, as well as a basis for orderly development of legal rules.*

Their lordships nevertheless recognise that the rigid adherence to precedent may lead to injustice in a particular case and also unduly restrict the proper development of the law. They propose therefore to modify their present practice and while treating former decisions of this house as normally binding, to depart from a previous decision when it appears right to do so.

In this connection they will bear in mind the danger of disturbing retrospectively the basis on which contracts, settlement of property and fiscal arrangements have been entered into and also the especial need for certainty as to the criminal law. This announcement is not intended to affect the use of precedent elsewhere in this house'

8

Court of appeal

The court of appeal is next in the hierarchy and has two divisions, civil and criminal. Both of these divisions are bound to follow the decisions of the European Court of Justice and the House of Lords. They must also follow past decisions of their own although there are exceptions to the rule and the Court of Appeal (Criminal Division) is more flexible where it involves the liberty of the subject.

Divisional courts

The three divisional courts, Queens bench, Chancery and Family are bound by decisions of the European Court of Justice, the House of Lords and the Court of Appeal. The divisional courts are also bound by their own past decisions, although there are some exceptions.

Courts of first instance

This term means any court where the original trial of a case is held. Appeal courts do not hear any original trials only appeals from those trials. Courts of first instance rarely ever create precedents only following decisions of courts above them.

The High Court

The High Court is bound by decisions of all courts above it and in turn it binds the lower courts.

Inferior courts

Inferior courts are the Crown Court, the County Court and the Magistrates Court. They are bound to follow decisions of all higher courts. It is very unlikely that a decision by a lower court can create a precedent. The one exception is that a ruling on a point of law by a judge in a Crown Court will bind the Magistrates Court.

Use of Practice Statement

Since 1966 the Practice Statement has allowed the House of Lords to Change the law if it believes that an earlier case was wrongly decided

Distinguishing, overruling and reversing previous decisions

Distinguishing is a method used by a judge to avoid following a past decision which otherwise would have to be followed. It means that the judge finds that the material facts of the case he is following are sufficiently different for him to draw a distinction between the present case and the previous case. He is not then bound by the previous case.

Overruling is where a court in a later case decides that the legal rule in a previous case is wrong. Overruling may occur when a higher court overrules a decision by a lower court, for example the House of Lords overruling a decision by the Court of Appeal.

Reversing is where a court higher up in the hierarchy overturns the decision of a lower court on appeal in the same case.

Advantages and disadvantages of precedent in the law

There are advantages and disadvantages to the way judicial precedent operates in England and Wales.

Advantages

The main advantages to the operation of precedent are:

Certainty
Because the courts follow past decisions, people know what the law is and how it is likely to be applied in their case. Lawyers advise clients on the likely outcome of cases and it also allows people to operate their businesses in the certainty that what they do is within the law.

Consistency and fairness
It is seen as just and fair that similar cases are decided in the same way.

Precision
As the principles of law are set out in actual cases, the law becomes very precise.

Flexibility
There is room for the law to change as the House of Lords can use the Practice Statement to overrule cases.

Time- saving
Precedent can be considered a useful time saving device as where a principle has been established, cases with similar facts are unlikely to go through the lengthy process of litigation.

Disadvantages

Rigidity
The fact that lower courts have to follow decisions of higher courts, together with the fact that the Court of Appeal has to follow its own past decisions, can make the law too inflexible so that bad decisions made in the past can be perpetuated.

Complexity
There are many reported cases and it may be complex and time consuming to find the right case on which to base a decision.

Illogical distinctions
The use of distinguishing to avoid past decisions can lead to illogical distinctions so that some areas of law have become very complex.

Reporting cases

Written law reports have existed in England and Wales since the 13th century. Reports right from the early times were inaccurate and difficult to follow. In 1865 the Incorporated Council of Law was set up, controlled by the courts. Law reports became more accurate and precise, with judgements being noted word for word.

This accuracy of reports was one of the factors in the development of the strict doctrine of precedent. There are also other well established reports today, notably the All England Series (abbreviated to All ER) and the weekly law Reports (WLR). The internet also provides reports, websites such as www. lawreports.co.uk and www.publications.parliament.uk.

3

Parliament and Acts of Parliament

The main legislative body in the United Kingdom is Parliament. Laws passed by Parliament are known as Acts of Parliament, or statutes. This source of law is usually referred to as statute law. In addition to Parliament, power is delegated to government ministers and their departments to make detailed rules and regulations which supplement Parliament. These regulations are delegated legislation and are called statutory instruments.

Parliament consists of the House of Commons and the House of Lords. Both houses must be in favour of a bill, vote in its favour, before it can become law.

The people who sit in the House of Commons are elected Members of Parliament, representing their constituencies who elected them.

The House of Lords is somewhat different consisting of hereditary peers, life peers, judges who are law lords and the most senior bishops in the Church of England. The Lords has, in the past few years, undergone radical reform with the process still continuing. Essentially, the process whereby hereditary peers dominated the Lords has ended with a more democratic approach being sought.

Judges in the House of Lords

As discussed, the House of Lords is the most senior court in England and Wales. The full title of this court is the Judicial Committee of the House of Lords. Only the 12 Law Lords are allowed to sit on this committee. There are proposals for a new supreme court to replace the Judicial Committee of the House of Lords so that judges will no longer sit in Parliament.

Factors influencing law making at a government level

When they are formed, Governments have programmes of reforms. These are set out in government manifestos at election time and reinforced during the Queens speech at the opening of Parliament. Basically, most new legislation emanates from government policy.
There are other influences at play which affect what laws are enacted. One such major influence is European legislation. New Acts are passed to bring our law in line with European legislation.

Other outside influences include proposals for law reform put forward by law reform agencies, commissions or enquiries into the effectiveness of existing law. Specific events can also lead to changes in the law, events such as the massacre of young children at a school in Dunblane in 1996 which resulted in Firearms Legislation in 1997.

Another outside influence is that of pressure groups who cause government to reconsider law in specific areas. One such instance was in 1994 when the government reduced the age of homosexual consent from 21 to 18. In 2000, this was further reduced to 16.

The pre-legislative process

On major matters a minister with responsibility for a specific area will issue a Green paper. This is a consultative document on a topic with the government's views on law reform. Following receipt of the views of all interested parties a White Paper will then be issued with its firm proposals for new law.

Introducing an Act of Parliament

The majority of Acts of Parliament are introduced by the government of the day. They are initially drafted by civil service lawyers known as Parliamentary Counsel to the Treasury.

When the proposed Act has been drafted it is published as a Bill. It will only progress to become an Act of Parliament if it completes all the stages successfully in Parliament. The drafting of Bills is painstaking and exact and must be framed in terms which are unambiguous. This is against a backdrop of the inevitable pressure of time.

Bills can also be sponsored by individual MP's. The Parliamentary process allows for a ballot in each session in which 20 private members are selected who can then take their turn in presenting a Bill to Parliament. Time for debate of these Bills is limited, usually being debated on a Friday and only a few members have a realistic chance of introducing a Bill on their chosen topic. Only a few Private Members Bills become law. Notable Acts passed have been the Abortion Act of 1967 which legalised abortion and the Marriage Act 1994 which allowed marriage in any registered place.

Backbenchers can also try to introduce a Bill through what is known as the 'Ten Minute Rule' under which any MP can make a speech of up to 10 minutes supporting the introduction of new legislation.

Members of the House of Lords can also introduce Private Members Bills.

The distinction between public and private Bills

A public Bill involves matters of public policy which will affect the country at large or a significant section of the country. Most Government Bills are in this category. However, some Bills are passed aimed at individuals or company's which are private Bills.

The Parliamentary process

In order for a Bill to become an Act of Parliament, it will usually have to be passed by both House of Commons and House of Lords. In each House there is a long process. A bill may commence in either House with the exception of finance Bills which must commence in the

Commons. There are a number of stages which all Bills must go through to become law:

1. First reading

This is a formal procedure where the name and aims of the Bill are read out. There will be a vote on whether the House wants to consider the Bill further. The vote can be verbal, where the speaker of the House asks the members as a whole how they vote and they shout out 'Aye' or 'No'. If it is clear that all members are in agreement, either for or against then there is no need for a formal vote. If it is not clear then a formal vote will be taken. Members of the House will leave the Chamber and then re-enter by one of two doors signifying for or against. Tellers total the votes for and against and declare the result to the Speaker.

2. Second reading

The second reading is the main debate on the whole Bill in which MP's debate the principles underlying the Bill. No one may speak without being called on to do so by the Speaker. At the end of the process a vote is taken in the same way as the first reading. To proceed to the next stage the Bill must be voted in favour of.

3. Committee stage

This stage is where a detailed examination of the Bill is undertaken by a committee of between 16 and 50 MP's. This is called a Standing Committee which is a committee chosen specifically to examine the Bill. This committee is made up by opposition and minority parties as well as the Government who will have a majority. Membership is made up in direct proportion to parties seats in the Houses of Parliament and will consist of people with a knowledge of the matter in hand.

4. Report stage

At the Committee stage amendments to various clauses in the Bill may have been voted on and passed. The report stage is where the Committee reports back to the House on the amendments.

5. Third reading

This stage is the final vote on the Bill. Having reached this stage it is unlikely to fail.

6. The House of Lords

If the Bill emanated from the Commons it will now go to the Lords where it will go through the same five stages and if amendments are made by the Lords to the Bill then it will go back to the Commons to consider those amendments. If the Bill emanated from the Lords then it will go to the Commons.

7. Royal assent

The final stage is where the monarch gives approval to the Bill and it then becomes an Act of Parliament. This is a formality. Under the Royal Assent Act 1961, the

Monarch will not even have the text of Bills to which she is assenting. She will only have the title of the Bill.

The diagram below summarises the process of legislation from drafting of a Bill to Act of Parliament through the House of Commons.

The Bill is Drafted

|

First reading in the House of Commons

|

Second reading in the House of Commons

|

Committee stage

|

Report stage

|

Third reading in the House of Commons

|

Same procedures in The House of Lords

|

Royal assent

The power of the House of Lords to reject a Bill is limited by the Parliament Acts of 1911 and 1949. These Acts allow a Bill to become law even if the Lords reject it provided that the Bill is re-introduced into the House of Commons in the next session of Parliament and goes through all the stages once again. The principle behind the Acts is that the House of Lords is not an elected body and its function is not to oppose the will of the elected House of Commons but to refine the law.

Commencement of an Act

Following Royal Assent the Act becomes law on midnight of that day, unless another date has been set for it to become law. This has become the norm, where a date is set where it should become law. A commencement order will be issued by the appropriate minister. In many cases, sections of an Act come into force at different times which causes confusion. This again is becoming something of a norm. One such Act was the Criminal Justice Act of 2003. At the time of writing there are still some sections of the Act not in force.

Parliamentary sovereignty

Parliamentary law is sovereign over other forms of law in England and Wales. This means that an Act of Parliament can completely supersede any custom, judicial precedent, delegated legislation or previous Act of Parliament. However, European law has undermined the sovereignty of Parliament in certain areas of law.

4

European Law

Since January 1st 1973, when the United Kingdom joined what was then the European Economic Community, set up by the Treaty of Rome in 1957, European law has gained an ever greater significance. Currently, there are 25 member states in the European Union. The European Union is a vast and complex organisation. The main institutions which exercise the functions of the EU are:

- The Council of the European Union
- The Commission
- The European Parliament
- The European Court of Justice

There are a number of ancillary bodies, the Economic and Social Committee being the most important.

The Council of Ministers

The government of each nation in the EU will send a representative to the Council. Usually the minister responsible for a particular area under discussion will attend. Twice a year, government heads meet in the European Council or Summit to discuss matters of policy. The member states take it in turns to provide the President of the Council, each for a six-month period. To assist with the day-to-day work of the council there is a committee of permanent representatives known as the *coreper*.

The Commission

The Commission consists of up to 30 Commissioners who are supposed to act independently. They are appointed for a five-year term and will head a specific department during their tenure. The Commission has several functions, proposing policies and presenting drafts of legislation to the Council. The Commission is also the 'guardian' of treaties. It ensures that treaty provisions adopted by the Council are properly implemented. It is also responsible for the administration of the Union.

The Assembly

The Assembly advises the Council and the Commission on economic matters. It is made up of representatives of influential interest groups such as farmers, employees and manufacturers. The Assembly must be consulted on proposed Union measures and has considerable influence on the decision making process.

The European Court of Justice

The function of the European Court of Justice is set out in Article 220 of the Treaty of Rome. This states that ' the Court must ensure that in the interpretation and application of the treaty the law is observed'.

The Court sits in Luxembourg and has 25 judges, one from each member state. Each judge is appointed for a term of six years and can be further reappointed. The Court is assisted by nine Advocates General who are also appointed for six years. Each case brought before the EU Court of Justice is given to an Advocates General whose task is to research all the appropriate legal points and to present a reasoned conclusion on cases to the Court.

The Courts main task is to ensure that the law is applied uniformly in all member states. It will hear cases to decide whether member states have failed to fulfil obligations under the Treaties. Such actions are usually initiated by the European Commission, although they can be started by another Member State.

The Court will also hear references from national courts for preliminary rulings on points of European law. Rulings made by the European Court of Justice are then binding on all Member States. This ensures that the law is uniform throughout Member States.

A request for a preliminary ruling is made under Article 234 of the Treaty of Rome. This states:

'the Court of Justice shall have jurisdiction to give preliminary rulings concerning:

    a) *the interpretation of Treaties;*
    b) *the validity and interpretation of Acts of the Institution of the Union;*
    c) *the interpretation of the statutes of bodies established by an Act of the Council, where those statutes so provide.*

Article 234 goes on to state that where there is no appeal from the national court within the national system, then courts must refer points of European law to the European Court of justice.

If this is applied to the court system in England and Wales, this means that the House of Lords must refer questions of European law, as it is the highest appeal court in our legal system. However, the Court of Appeal does not have to refer questions.

However, even courts at the bottom of the system can refer questions of law under Article 234 if they feel that a preliminary ruling is necessary to enable a judgement in a particular case to be given. The European Court will not decide such a case only make a preliminary ruling and then refer the case back to the court in question.

Discretionary referrals

The Court of Appeal set out its approach to discretionary referrals in the case of Bulmer v Bollinger (1974). The guidelines are as follows:

- Guidance on a point of law must be necessary to come to a decision in a case
- There is no need to refer a question which has already been decided by the European Union in a previous case
- There is no need to refer a point which is reasonably clear and free from doubt
- The court must consider all the circumstances of the case

- The English court retains the discretion on whether to refer or not

The Court of First Instance

This was set up in 1988 to relieve the European Court of Justice of some of its workload. This court hears cases between European institutions and their employees. It also hears complex economic cases in the field of competition law, 'anti-dumping' law and under the European Coal and Steel Treaty. This court has 12 judges.

Regulations

Under Article 249 of the Treaty of Rome, the European Union has the power to issue regulations which are binding in every respect and directly applicable to every Member state. Such regulations do not have to be adopted by Member States as they automatically become law in each member country.

Directives

Directives are the main way in which harmonisation of laws within Member states is achieved. There have been directives covering a whole range of topics, such as company law, banking, insurance employment and consumer law. As with regulations, Article 249 of the Treaty of Rome gives the power to the Union to issue directives. Article 249 states directives:

' *bind any Member state to which they are addressed as to the result to be achieved, while leaving to domestic agencies a competence as to form and means'*

This means that Member states will pass their own laws to bring directives into effect. The usual method of implementing directives in the United Kingdom is by Statutory Instrument. One key example of this was the Unfair Terms in Consumer Contracts Regulations 1994. The time-frame for implementation is set by the European Commission.

Where Member states have not implemented a directive within the time set out by the Commission, the European Court of Justice has developed the concept of 'direct effect'. This means that a directive may be directly enforceable by an individual by a member state. This will be the case even though a Member state has not implemented the directive or has implemented it incorrectly. The main point here is that the individual who is affected only has rights against the state. This is because of the concepts of vertical and horizontal effect.

Vertical effect

Vertical direct effect was illustrated effectively in the case of Marshall v Southampton and South West Area health Authority (1986). The facts were that Miss Marshall was required to retire from her post at the age of 62. Men doing the same work did not have to retire until the age of 65. Under the Sex Discrimination Act of 1976 in English Law, this was not discriminatory. However, Miss Marshall succeeded in her action for unfair dismissal by relying on the Equal Treatment Directive 76/207. This directive had not been fully implemented in the United Kingdom but the European Court of Justice held that it was sufficiently clear and imposed obligations on a Member State. This ruling allowed Miss Marshall to succeed in her action against her employers because they were an arm of the state, i.e. they were considered as part of the state. The directive had vertical effect allowing her to rely on it to take action against them. The concept of state is quite wide, as it was ruled by the European Court of Justice in Foster v British Gas plc (1990) that the state was:

'a body, whatever its legal form, which has been made responsible, pursuant to a measure adopted by the State, for providing a public service under the control of the State and has for that purpose special powers beyond those which result from the normal rules applicable in relations between individuals'.

Horizontal direct effect

Directives which have not been implemented do not give an individual any rights against other people. As seen they are only applicable in cases against the state.

The conflict between European law and national law

Inevitably there will be conflict between national and European law. European law takes precedence over national law. This was first established in Van Gend en Loos (1963) which involved a conflict of Dutch law and European law on customs duty. The Dutch Government argued that the European Court of Justice had no jurisdiction to decide whether European law would prevail over Dutch law. However, the European Court rejected this argument. In Costa v ENEL (1964) the European Court decided that even if there was a later national law this did not take precedence over EU law.

5

Statutory Interpretation of the Law

In many cases, there are disputes over the meaning of Acts of Parliament. Although Acts will have interpretive sections allowing for broader interpretations of the Act there is, in many cases, still confusion.

In cases such as the above it is the courts role to interpret the Act and decide the exact meaning of a particular word, group of words or a phrase. The reasons why a meaning can be unclear are many and include the fact that broad terms have been used to cover several possibilities, there is ambiguity, error in drafting, new developments rendering older Acts of Parliament obsolete, changes in the use of language and so on. For all these reasons and more, sometimes the courts are called on to interpret an Act.

Literal approach versus Purposive approach

One of the major problems concerning statutory interpretation is that of whether the judge in a case should take each word in an Act and interpret it literally or whether he/she should go beyond the literal meaning and take a more purposive approach, accept that words cannot cover all situations and look at the facts of the case more closely. In English law judges have not been able to agree on which approach to adopt. However, over the years they have developed three different rules of interpretation:

- The literal rule
- The golden rule
- The mischief rule

We will discuss each one in turn.

The literal rule

Under this rule courts will give words their plain, ordinary or literal meaning, even if the end result of such an interpretation is undesirable and not very sensible. This idea was expressed by Lord Esher in R v Judge of the City of London Court (1892) when he said:

' *if the words of an Act are clear then you must follow them even though they lead to a manifest absurdity. The court has nothing to do with the question whether the legislature has committed an absurdity'.*

The rule above has been used since the early nineteenth century and in many cases the outcome has been nonsense.

The golden rule

This rule is a modification of the literal rule. The golden rule starts by looking at the literal meaning but the court is then allowed to arrive at an interpretation which avoids absurdity.

The mischief rule

This rule gives the judge more discretion than the literal or golden rules. The definition of the mischief rule comes from the Heydon's case (1584) where it was said that there were four points the court should consider. These (couched in the original language) were:

1. What was the common law before the making of the Act?
2. What was the mischief and defect for which the common law did not provide?
3. What was the remedy the Parliament hath resolved and appointed to cure the disease of the commonwealth?
4. The true reason of the remedy.
   Then the office of all judges is always to make such construction as shall suppress the mischief and advance the remedy.

Under this rule therefore, the court should look to see what the law was before the Act was passed in order to discover what gap, or 'mischief' the Act was intended to cover. The court should then interpret the Act in such a way that the gap is covered.

Rules of language

Even the literal rule does not take cases in complete isolation. Other words in the Act must be looked at to see if they affect the word or phrase which is in dispute. In looking at other words the courts have developed a set of rules:

- The *ejusdem generis* rule
- The express mention of one thing excludes others
- A word is known by the company it keeps

The *ejusdem generis* rule

This rule states that where there is a list of words followed by general words, then the general words are limited to the same kind of items as the specific words. If we look at the case of *Powell v Kempton park Racecourse* (1899) the defendant was charged with 'keeping a house, an office, room or other place for betting'. He had been operating betting at what was known as Tattersall's Ring, which is outside. The court decided that the general words 'other place' had to refer to indoor places since all words in the list were indoor places so the defendant was not guilty.

There must be at least two specific words in a list for this rule to operate.

Expressio Unius Exclusio Alterius (the mention of one thing excludes others

Where there is a list of words which is not followed by general words, then the Act applies only to the items in the list. In *Tempest v Kilner* (1846) the court had to consider whether the Statute of Frauds 1677 (which required a contract for the sale of goods, wares and merchandise, of more than £10 to be evidenced in writing) applied to a contract for the sale of stocks and shares. The list 'goods, wares and merchandise, was not followed by any general words, so the court decided that only contracts for three types of things were affected by the statute: because the stocks and shares were not mentioned they were not caught by the statute.

NOSCITUR A SOCIIS (a word is known by the company it keeps)

This means that the words must be looked at in context and interpreted accordingly. It involves looking at words in the same section or other section of the Act. One case which illustrates this is *Inland Revenue Commissioners v Frere* (1965) where the section set out rules for 'interest, annuities or other annual interest'. The first use of the word 'interest' on its own could have meant any interest paid, whether daily, monthly or annually. Because of the words 'other annual interest' in the section, the court decided that 'interest' only meant annual interest.

Presumptions

The courts will also make certain presumptions about the law. If the statute clearly states the opposite, then the presumption will not apply and it is said that the presumption is rebutted. The most important presumptions are: a presumption against a change in the common law, i.e. a presumption that the common law has not changed unless Parliament has changed it in an Act; a presumption that *mens rea* is required in a criminal case. The basic common law rule is that no-one can be convicted of a crime unless it is shown that they had the intention to commit it.

There will also be a presumption that the Crown is not bound by any statute unless the statute expressly says so. There will be a presumption that legislation does not apply retrospectively.

Unified approach to interpretation

Looking at all these approaches the question is raised, how do they all fit together. The unified approach, according to Sir Rupert Cross, is thus:
1. A judge should start by using the grammatical and ordinary or, where appropriate, technical meaning of the words in the general context of the statute.
2. If the judge considers that this would produce an absurd result, then he may apply any secondary meaning, which the words are capable of bearing.
3. The judge may read in words which he considers to be necessarily implied by the words which are in the statute, and he has a limited power to add to, alter or ignore words in order to prevent a provision from being unintelligible, unworkable or absurd.
4. In applying these rules the judge may resort to the various aids and presumptions.

The purposive approach

Using this approach, judges will decide what they believe Parliament meant to achieve. The major exponent of this approach was Lord Denning. In the case of Magor and St Mellons v Newport Corporation (1950) he said:

' We sit here to find out the intention of Parliament and carry it out, and we do this better by filling in the gaps and making sense of the enactment than by opening it up to destructive analysis'.

There have been many criticisms of the purposive approach, with judges stating that it is up to the courts not to interpret legislation but to follow the enactment. If any amendments need to be made they should be made by amending the Act.

6

The Legal Profession

In the English Legal System, there are two types of lawyers, Barristers and Solicitors.

The Law Society oversees the activities of solicitors as well as the legal profession as a whole. The General Council of the Bar oversees Barristers.

Solicitors

To become a solicitor it is usual to either have a law degree or have completed an extra year of law if the degree is a non-law degree. This is called the Common Professional Examination.

When the course has been completed successfully the student is still not a solicitor. A training contract must be obtained from a firm of solicitors and two years work must be completed. This training period can also be undertaken in other legal organisations such as the Crown Prosecution Service, or the legal department of a local authority. During the training period he or she will have to undertake their own work and complete a 20 day Professional Skills Course after which time the person will be admitted as a solicitor by the Law Society. Even after qualifying, solicitors have to attend continuing education to keep their skills up to date.

There is a non-graduate route to become a solicitor for mature candidates but the process takes longer to complete.

Solicitors who qualify will either work in private practice in a solicitors firm, or can work for the Crown Prosecution Service or for a local authority or government department. Some will become legal advisors to big companies.

Solicitors will work in sole practices or partnerships and the type of work carried out will be varied depending largely on the specialism of the firm. A small firm will usually cover a whole range of matters from housing, family, conveyancing and business matters. It is usual for a solicitor to specialise in a particular area.

All solicitors can act as advocates in the Magistrates Court. After 1986 solicitors can appear in a High Court to make a statement after a case has been settled.

Complaints against solicitors

A client can sue a solicitor for negligence in and out of court work. One case where this happened was Griffiths v Dawson (1993) where solicitors for the plaintiff failed to make a correct application in divorce proceedings against her husband. As a result of this the plaintiff lost financially and the solicitors were ordered to pay £21,000 compensation.

Office for the Supervision of Solicitors

The Office for the Supervision of Solicitors was set up in 1996 to deal with complaints against solicitors. It is funded by the Law Society.

Barristers

Collectively, barristers are referred to as 'the Bar' and they are controlled by their own professional body-the General Council of the Bar. All barristers must also be a member of one of the four Inns of Court, Lincolns Inn, Inner Temple, Middle Temple and Gray's Inn all of which are situated near the Royal Courts of Justice in London.

Entry to the Bar is usually degree based although a small number of mature entrants can qualify. As with solicitor's graduates with a non-law degree can take a one-year course for the Common Professional Examination in the core subjects in order to qualify as a barrister. All student barristers must pass the Bar Vocational Course which emphasises the practical skills of drafting pleadings for use in court negotiation and advocacy.

All student barristers must join one of the four Inns of Court Until 1997, it was mandatory to dine there 12 times before being called to the Bar. However, students may now attend in a different way, such as a weekend residential course.

After being called to the Bar a Barrister must complete a practical stage of the training called pupillage. This is on-the-job training where the trainee barrister becomes a pupil to a qualified barrister. This involves shadowing the barrister and can be with the same barrister for 12 months or with two barristers for six months each. There is also a requirement to take part in ongoing continuing education organised by the Bar Council. After the first six months of pupillage barristers can appear on their own in court.

Barristers practicing at the Bar are self-employed but share the administrative expenses of a set of chambers. Most sets of chambers comprise 15-29 barristers. They will employ a clerk as an administrator. The majority of barristers will concentrate on advocacy, although there are some who will specialise.

Originally, it was necessary for anyone who wanted to instruct a barrister to go to a solicitor first. The solicitor would then brief the barrister. After September 2004, it has been possible for anyone to contact barristers direct. However, direct access is still not allowed for criminal work or family work.

Barristers can be employed direct (the employed bar) working for example, for the Crown Prosecution Service and can represent in court.

Queen's Counsel

After a Barrister or solicitor has served at least 16 years with an advocacy qualification, it is then possible to become a Queens Counsel (QC). About 10% of the Bar are Queens Counsel and it is known as 'taking silk'. QC's usually take on complicated, high profile cases.

Until 2004 Queen's Counsel were appointed by the Lord Chancellor. After 2004, selection is by a panel chaired by a non-lawyer. Selection is by interview and applicants can provide references.

Complaints against barristers

Where a barrister receives a brief from a solicitor he or she does not enter into a contract with a client and so cannot sue if fees are not paid. Likewise the client cannot sue for breach of contract. However, they can be sued for negligence. In the case Saif Ali v Sydney Mitchell and Co (1990) it was held that a barrister could be sued for negligence in respect of written advice and opinions. In that particular case a barrister had given wrong advice on who to sue, with the result that the claimant was too late to start proceedings against the right person.

Solicitors and barristers summarised

	Solicitors	Barristers
Professional body	Law Society	Bar Council
Basic qualifications	Law degree or non-law degree with one years Common Professional Exam	Law degree or non-law degree with one years Common Professional Exam
Vocational	Legal practice	Bar vocational

training	course	course
Practical training	Training contract	Pupillage
Methods of working	Firm of partners or sole practitioner	Self-employed Practicing in Chambers
Rights of audience	Normally only County Court and Magistrates Court	All courts
Relationship with client	Contractual	Normally through solicitor but Accountants and Surveyors can Brief barristers directly
Liability	Liable in contract and tort to clients may also be liable to others affected by negligence	No contractual liability but liable for negligence

The Judiciary

Collectively, judges are known as the judiciary. The head of the Judiciary is the Lord Chancellor.

Types of judges

Superior judges

Superior judges are those in the high court and above. These are (from top to bottom):

- The Lords of Appeal in Ordinary (the Law Lords) in the House of Lords
- The Lords Justices of Appeal in the Court of Appeal
- High Court Judges (known as puisne judges) who sit in the three divisions of the High Court

The head of the House of Lords is the Lord Chancellor. Specific posts heading the different divisions of the Court of Appeal and the High Court are:

- The Lord Chief Justice, who is the president of the Criminal Division of the Court of Appeal and the senior judge in the Queens Bench Division of the High Court
- The Master of the Rolls who is president of the Civil Division of the Court of Appeal
- The President of the Family Division of the High Court
- The Vice Chancellor of the Chancery Division of the High Court

Inferior judges

The inferior judges are:

- Circuit judges who sit in both the Crown Court and the County Court
- Recorders who are part-time judges sitting usually in the Crown Court though some may be assigned to the County Court

- District judges who hear small claims and other matters in the County Court
- District judges (Magistrates Court) who sit in Magistrates Courts in the major towns and cities
- Chairmen of Tribunals

To become a judge at any level it is necessary to have qualified as a barrister or solicitor. It is not essential to have practiced, as the Courts and Legal Services Act 1990 provided for academic lawyers to be appointed.

Law Lords

Law lords are appointed from those who hold high judicial office, for example as a judge in the Court of Appeal. As the House of Lords is the final appellate court in Scotland and Northern Ireland as well, judges can also be appointed from those who have practiced as an advocate in Scotland for at Least 15 years or as a Member of the Bar in Northern Ireland for at least 15 years or have held high judicial office in their own legal system.

Lords Justices of Appeal

Lords Justices of Appeal must have a 10 year High Court Qualification or be an existing High Court Judge.

High Court Judges

To be eligible to be a High Court Judge it is necessary either to have had the right to practice in the High Court for 10 years or more or to have been a Circuit Judge for at least 2 years. New qualifications give solicitors the chance to become High Court Judges. It is also possible for academic lawyers who have not practiced as barristers or solicitors to be appointed.

Circuit judges

To become a circuit judge a candidate can either have had rights of audience for 10 years or more in either the Crown Court or County Court or to have been a recorder. The Courts and Legal Services Act 1990 also allows for promotion after being a district judge, stipendiary magistrate or chairman of an employment tribunal for at least three years.

Recorders

A Recorder is a part-time post. The applicant must have practiced as a barrister or solicitor for at least 10 years.

District judges

District judges need a seven year general qualification. They are appointed from either barristers or solicitors. District judges in the Magistrates Court need the same qualification.

Law Officers

There is a law office within government that advises on matters of law that affects government. There are two law officers: the Attorney General and the Solicitor General. Both are members of the government of the day and are appointed by the Prime Minister. Both will usually be Members of the House of Commons. The Attorney General appoints the Director of Public Prosecutions, who heads the Crown Prosecution Service.

The Attorney General

The Attorney General is the Government's chief legal advisor. He is not a member of the main cabinet. He will advise government on legislative proposals and on criminal proceedings which have a political or public element. He is also responsible for major litigation which involves the government.

The Attorney General is appointed from those members of Parliament who are barristers and he can represent the government in court proceedings. He is the head of the English Bar but cannot practice privately as a barrister.

The Attorney General's consent is required before a prosecution can commence in certain cases such as corruption, possessing explosive substances and hijacking. He can grant immunity from prosecution and can stop proceedings for an indictable offence. He can also instruct the Director of Public Prosecutions to take over any private prosecution.

The Attorney General has the right to refer any criminal cases to the Court of Appeal (Criminal Division) for a point of law to be considered following an acquittal in the Crown Court and he can appeal against a sentence which is considered too lenient.

The Solicitor General

The Solicitor General acts as a deputy to the Attorney General.

The Director of Public Prosecutions

The DPP's duties are set out in the Prosecution of Offences Act 1985, which created the Crown Prosecution Service. The DPP must be a barrister or solicitor of at least 10 years standing. The appointment is made by the Attorney General to whom the DPP is accountable. The main function of the DPP is to head the Crown Prosecution Service. The other functions are set out in the Prosecution of Offences Act 1985, which are:

- To take over the conduct of all criminal proceedings instituted by the police
- To institute and oversee the conduct of criminal proceedings where the importance of difficulty of the proceedings makes this appropriate
- To take over the conduct of binding over proceedings brought by the police
- To give advice to police forces on all matters relating to criminal offences
- To appear for the prosecution in certain appeals

Magistrates
Lay magistrates
Lay magistrates, other wise known as Justices of the Peace sit to hear cases as a bench of two or three magistrates. Single magistrates can issue search warrants and warrants for arrest.

71

Lay magistrates do not have to have any qualifications in law. They must, however, be suitable in character and integrity and also have an understanding of the work that they perform. There are formal requirements as to age and residence and a magistrate must live within the area where they will sit: lay magistrates must be aged between 18 and 65 on appointment.

Some people are not eligible to be appointed, including people with a serious criminal record, though minor offences such as driving offences will not disqualify a person. Others who are disqualified are undischarged bankrupts, members of the forces and those whose work is not compatible with sitting as a magistrate, such as police officers.

About 1,500 new lay magistrates are appointed each year, by the Lord Chancellor.

Duties of magistrates

Magistrates have a wide workload mainly connected to criminal cases, although they also deal with civil matters. The criminal cases involve early administrative hearings, remand hearings, bail applications and committal proceedings. They also deal with debt related civil matters such as non-payment of utility bills, council tax etc. In addition, they will also hear appeals relating to the refusal of the local authority to grant licences for the sale of alcohol and for betting and gaming establishments.

Specially trained justices will form the Youth Court to hear criminal charges against young offenders aged from

10-17years old. There is also a special panel to hear cases including orders for protection against violence, affiliation cases, adoption orders and proceedings under the Children Act 1989.

Lay magistrates also sit at the Crown Court to hear appeals from the Magistrates Court. In these cases the lay justices form a panel with a qualified judge.

The magistrates clerk

Every bench of magistrates is assisted by a clerk. The senior clerk in each court has to be qualified as a barrister or solicitor for at least five years. The clerk's duty is to advise the magistrates on questions of law, practice and procedure. The Crime and Disorder Act 1998 also gives clerks the powers to deal with Early Administrative Hearings.

7

Civil cases

We have already discussed the difference between civil cases and criminal cases. Civil cases are between individuals (including companies) and criminal cases involve the state against others.

The types of disputes that can arise in civil cases are varied. The claim can be for money, from relatively small amounts to huge amounts. Contract law is involved. An individual may be claiming compensation for injury or some other form of injustice (tort). Other types of orders sought may be for injunctions to prevent someone from doing something or the winding up of a company or divorce following a failed marriage. Civil cases are of a wide variety. In this chapter we discuss the workings of the civil courts.

Taking a case to court is expensive unless the party to a case is prepared to go down the do-it-yourself route. However, prior to going to court it is expected by the courts that some form of negotiation has taken place. Failure to do so is looked at in a dim light by any judge.

Commencing a court case in the county courts

The civil court system has undergone significant reform since the Woolf Report of 1999. Parties to a case are encouraged to give information to each other to prevent the need to go to court in the first place. This is seen as a way of ensuring that the court system does not get clogged up with unnecessary cases. Before an action is commenced and a claim is issued, a pre-action protocol should be followed. This, basically, is a list of things that should be done and if the parties to a case or potential case do not follow a procedure and give the required information to the other party, they may be liable for certain costs if they then make a court claim.

This information will usually be in the form of a letter explaining how the claim has arisen, why it is claimed that the other party is at fault, details of the injury or other damage and anything else relevant to the case. The defendant is then given three months to respond and investigate the claim admitting or denying the claim. If any other evidence is needed, such as expert evidence then the parties should agree on one expert. If this does not solve matters then it may still be necessary to go to court.

Commencing a court case

Which court?

If a decision has been made to go to court then the question will be which court? As discussed, the two courts which hear civil cases are the county court and the high court. For cases where the claim is for £15,000 or less, the case must be started in the county court. For claims larger than this amount the High court or county court can be used. There are however, some restrictions laid down as to the use of courts in the High Court and County Courts Jurisdiction Order 1991. These are that personal injury cases for less than £50,000 must be started in the county court and defamation actions must commence in the High Court.

The main consideration when commencing a claim over £15,000 is how complex the case is going to be. If it is fairly straightforward then it should commence in the county court if it is complex then the High Court should be used.

Issuing a claim against another party

If the county court is to be used, then the claim can be issued in any of the county courts in the country. If the High Court is to be used then you can go to one of the 20 District Registries or the main court in London. You will need to use a claim form called an 'N1'. The court office will supply notes on how to fill in the form. There is a fee for commencing the case and the courts will advise you of this.

Defending a claim

When a claim form is received by a defendant there are several alternatives courses of action. The defendant can admit the claim and settle. When this happens the case ends. If the claim is defended he or she may serve an acknowledgement of service (form N9) or a defence to the court within 14 days of receiving the claim. If only an acknowledgement of service is sent then the defendant has an extra 14 days to serve the defence.

If the defendant does not respond at all, the claimant can ask the court to make an order that the defendant pays the monies owed and also costs of the claim. This is called an order in default. If the case is defended then the court will allocate the case to the most suitable 'track' .

The decision on which track to be used is made by the District Judge in the county court or the Master (a procedural judge) in the High Court. The tracks are:

- The small claims track. This is normally used for disputes under £5,000, except for personal injury and housing cases where the limit is lower, usually £1,000
- The fast track. This is normally used for straightforward disputes of £5,000-£15,000.
- The multi-track. This is for cases over £15,000 or for complex cases under this amount.

Both parties will be sent an allocation questionnaire in order to assist the judge in deciding which track to allocate the case to. Judge can also make a decision to transfer cases from one court to another.

The Small claims track

As stated, the small claims track deals with cases of £5,000 or under. People are encouraged to take their own cases so that costs are kept to a minimum. The actual process of commencing a claim is relatively simple, being paper driven. Most major towns will have a county court and addresses can be found in libraries or on the internet. These courts can hear nearly all civil cases, the main types being contract and tort cases, cases for recovery of land, disputes over partnerships, trusts and inheritance up to £30,000, divorce cases, bankruptcy, admiralty cases and matters under the Race Relations Act 1976.

The county court can try small claims, fast track and multi track cases. Cases will almost always be heard in open court and members of the public are entitled to attend. The exceptions to this are matters of a more personal nature such as family matters. Cases are heard by circuit judges.

Fast-track cases

Cases of between £5000 and £15,000 are allocated to the fast track. Personal injury cases and housing cases of between £1000 and £15,000 are also heard fast-track. Fast-track means that the court will set out a very rigid timetable for the pre-trial matters. Once a case is set down for hearing the aim is for the case to be heard within 30 weeks.

The actual trial will be heard by a circuit judge and the pre-trial hearing will last no longer than one day.

Multi-track cases

Claims for more than £15,000 are normally allocated to the multi-track. If the case was commenced in a county court then it will usually be heard there, although it can be sent to the High Court, especially if the claim is over £50,000.

The High Court

This court is based in London but has branches in 26 towns and cities throughout England and Wales. It has the power to hear any civil case and consists of three divisions each of which specialises in hearing a specific type of case: The Queens Bench Division, The Chancery Division and the Family Division.

The Queens Bench Division

The President of the Queens Bench Division is the Lord Chief Justice with up to 70 judges sitting in this division. It deals with contract and tort cases where the amount being claimed exceeds £50,000. As we have seen, a claimant can start an action for £15,000 and above. The High Court will only deal with multi-track cases. There is a right to jury in cases for fraud, libel, slander, malicious prosecution and false imprisonment cases. The role of the jury is discussed later in the book.

Commercial court

This is part of the Queens Bench division with specialist judges who will listen to commercial cases such as insurance and banking.

Admiralty court

This court deals with shipping and deciding such matters as collisions at sea and salvage rights. In 1998, the Technology and Construction Court was set up to deal with complex building and engineering disputes.

The Queens Bench Division also has an important supervisory function over inferior courts, and other bodies with decision-making powers, such as government ministers and local councils. The process of judicial review concerns itself with whether a decision making process has been carried out legally.

The Chancery Division

The Lord Chancellor assisted by the Vice Chancellor is the head of the Chancery Division. The main business of this division involves disputes with matters such as insolvency, the enforcement of mortgages, disputes relating to trust property, copyright and patents, intellectual property and contested probate. There is also a special companies court dealing with winding up companies.

Family division

The head of the Family Division is the President and 17 High Court Judges are assigned to this division. It hears all wardship cases and all cases relating to children under the Children Act 1989. It also deals with all other family matters, such as declarations of nullity of marriage, and grants probate in non-contentious probate cases.

The Civil Procedure Rules

From 26th April 1999, new Civil Procedure Rules came into effect. Rule 1.1 of the CPR states that the overriding objective is to enable the court to deal with cases justly.

Under the CPR the terminology has changed to make the whole process more user friendly. For example, the word 'plaintiff' has been changed to claimant. Courts should try to:

- ensure that parties in any case are on an equal footing
- Save expense
- Deal with cases in a way which is proportionate to;

  -the amount involved (avoid costs exceeding amount claimed

  -the importance of the case

  -the complexity of the case
- Ensure that the case is dealt with quickly and fairly
- Allocate an appropriate share of the courts resources.

Judges now have more control over cases than they used to, setting out timetables for cases and eliminating time wasting and actively managing cases including identifying issues at an early stage and encouraging parties to use alternative dispute resolution.

Appellate Courts
These are courts which hear appeals from lower courts. The main appellate courts are the Divisional Courts, the Court of Appeal and the House of Lords.

Divisional Courts
Each division of the High Court has a divisional court which has the power to hear appeals from inferior courts and tribunals.

Queens Bench Divisional Court

This is the most important of the Divisional Courts and has two main functions:

1. It hears appeals by way of case stated from criminal cases decided in the Magistrates Court.
2. It has supervisory powers over inferior courts and tribunals and also over the actions and decisions of public bodies and Government ministers. This is known as Judicial Review, as previously discussed.

The Queens Bench Divisional Court also hears matters relating to unlawful detainment and the right to liberty.

Chancery Divisional Court

The Chancery Divisional Court deals with a small number of appeals, mainly tax related appeals and appeals arising from bankruptcy cases.

Family Divisional Court

This court hears appeals from the decisions of magistrates regarding family matters and orders affecting children.

Court of Appeal (Civil Division)

The Court of Appeal has two divisions, civil and criminal. There are 35 Lord Justices of Appeal. The Civil Division is the main appellate court for civil cases and it is headed by the Master-of-the-Rolls. The Court of Appeal (Civil Division) mainly hears appeals from the following courts:

- All three divisions of the High Court
- The County Court for multi-track cases
- The Immigration Appeal Tribunal
- Some tribunals

Permission to appeal is required in most cases. It can be granted by the court where the decision was made, or by the Court of Appeal. Permission to appeal is only granted where the court feels that an appeal may have some success or there is some other reason why the appeal should be heard.

Permission to appeal is not required where the liberty of an individual is at stake.

The House of Lords

This is the final and highest court of appeal in the English legal system. It hears appeals from the Court of Appeal, the Divisional Courts and in rare cases from the High Court.

Appeal routes in civil cases

Appeals from the County Court
The appeal routes from the County Court are set out in Part 52 of the Civil Procedure Rules. Generally:

- fast track cases dealt with by a District judge-these appeals are heard by a Circuit Judge
- For fast track cases dealt with by a circuit judge the appeal is heard by a High Court Judge
- For final decisions in multi track cases heard in the County Court the right of appeal is to the Court of Appeal

Appeals from small claims

After October 2000 appeals against decisions in small claims cases became possible. The appeal routes are the same as for fast track cases.

Appeals from the High Court

From a decision in the High Court the appeal will go to the Court of Appeal (Civil Division). In rare cases there may be a leapfrog decision to the House of Lords under the Administration of Justice Act 1969.

Further appeals

From a decision of the Court of Appeal there is a further appeal to the House of Lords but only if the House of Lords or Court of Appeal gives its permission to appeal. If a point of European law is involved the case may be referred to the European Court of Justice. This referral can be made by an English Court.

Remedies in civil cases
The main remedy awarded by the courts is an order for financial recompense. This is termed an award of

damages. The object of awarding financial damages, in contract cases, is to put the claimant in a position, as far as possible where they may have been if the breach had not occurred. This will be the same in negligence (tort) cases.

Special damages

These will be damages which can be specifically calculated. One such example may be the cost of repairing a car after a crash.

General damages

These are for areas that cannot be so readily calculated and itemised. Personal injury cases can involve pain and suffering and the amount of general damages will include the costs of future care and provision.

Nominal damages

Where a case is won but loss cannot be demonstrated the courts will be in a position to award nominal damages in recognition of an individuals rights being infringed.

Exemplary damages

These are also termed 'punitive damages'. They are damages that are intended to punish the defendant, not only compensate the claimant. Exemplary damages are not available for breach of contract and are only awarded in tort cases where they are authorised by statute, where there has been oppressive, arbitrary or unconstitutional action by servants of the government. In addition, they are awarded where the defendant intended to make a profit from the tort which would be greater than the compensation due from the tort.

Equitable remedies

The major equitable remedies are injunctions, specific performance and rescission.

Injunctions

Temporary injunctions, called interlocutory injunctions can be granted during the course of a case This is usually granted in order to preserve the status quo between then parties while the case is awaiting a full trial.

Injunctions are used in many areas of law, contract, family and employment. Breach of an injunction is a contempt of court.

Specific performance

This is a remedy only used in contract law and it is an order that a contract should only be carried out as agreed.

Rescission

This is also only available in contract cases. The aim of rescission is to return the parties to their pre-contractual position. The main ground for rescission is a misrepresentation, which caused one party to enter into a contract erroneously.

Rectification

This is a court order that a document should be altered to reflect the party's intention.

Alternative Dispute Resolution

As we have seen, using courts to solve civil cases is costly, or can be, and takes time. As a result, many people use what is knows as Alternative Dispute Resolution (ADR) in order to arrive at a solution to their problems.

In employment cases, ADR has long been used, primarily through ACAS (Advisory, Conciliation and Arbitration Service) Neutral mediators are used in some cases. However, this is only useful if there is a hope of parties to a dispute agreeing. There are a growing number of mediation services, one of the main ones being the Centre for Dispute Resolution set up in 1991.

Conciliation is similar to mediation in that there will be a third party helping to resolve the issues. Conciliators play a more active role generally than mediators.

8

Criminal cases

Over time, there has been a general increase in recorded crime, with violent crime on the increase. The police are obviously in the front line dealing with crime as a whole. The main police powers are contained within the Police and Criminal Evidence Act (PACE) 1984 with amendments and additions made by the Criminal Justice and Public Order Act 1994 and the Criminal Justice Act 2003. PACE also provides for the codes of practice giving extra details on the procedures for stop and search, detaining, questioning and identifying suspects. These are issued by the Home Secretary.

Police powers

The police have to exercise their powers sensitively and respect the rights of the individual citizen. At the same time they must also have sufficient powers to enable them to do their job.

The law on police powers is mainly contained within the Police and Criminal Evidence Act 1984 and the associated codes of practice contained within section 66 of the act. There are six codes:

- Code A deals with the powers to stop and search

- Code B for the powers to search premises and seize property
- Code C deals with detention, treatment and questioning of subjects
- Code D deals with the rules for identification procedures
- Code E deals with the tape recording of interviews with suspects
- Code F deals with visual recording of interviews

Powers to arrest-serious arrestable offences

Some of the rules only apply to serious arrestable offences. These include murder, treason, manslaughter, rape, hijacking, kidnapping, hostage taking, drug trafficking, firearms offences and causing explosions likely to endanger life or property. Other arrestable offences may only be considered to be serious if they endanger the state or public order or cause death of a person.

Powers to stop and search

The powers of police to stop and search people or vehicles are contained in sections 1-7 of PACE. Section 1 gives police the powers to stop and search people and vehicles in a public place. A public place has a wide meaning and extends to private gardens if the police officer in question has good reason to believe that the suspect does not live at that address. To use this power under PACE the police officer must have reasonable grounds for suspecting that the person is in possession of stolen goods or prohibited articles or goods. These include knives and other weapons which can cause harm or be used in burglary or theft.

Voluntary searches

This is where a person is prepared to submit to a search voluntarily. A voluntary search can only take place where there is power to search anyway. Voluntary searches must be recorded.

Other powers to stop and search

Apart from PACE there are also other Acts of Parliament which give the police the right to stop and search in special circumstances. The Misuse of Drugs Act 1971 allows the police to search for controlled drugs and the Terrorism Act 2000 gives powers to stop and search where there is reasonable suspicion of involvement in terrorism.

Section 60 of the Criminal Justice and Public Order Act 1994 gives the police an additional power of the right to stop and search in anticipation of violence.

Roadside checks

Section 4 of PACE gives police the right to stop and search vehicles if there is a reasonable suspicion that a person who has committed a serious offence is at large in an area.

The power to search premises

In certain circumstances the police have the power to enter and search premises. PACE sets out most of these powers although there are other Acts which provide for this mentioned later.

The police can enter a premises without the occupiers permission if a warrant authorising that search has been obtained from a magistrate. This will normally be issued under section 8 of PACE. The magistrate must be convinced that the police have reasonable grounds for believing that a serious arrestable offence has been committed and that there is material on the premises that will be of substantial value in the investigation of the offence.

Search warrants are designed to enable the element of surprise and in the process prevent valuable evidence being removed or destroyed.

A warrant must specify the premises to be searched and, as far as possible, the articles or persons to be sought. One entry only, on one occasion is authorised and entry must be at a reasonable hour unless the police can demonstrate the need to enter at another time. They are also required to identify themselves as police officers and to show the warrant on demand.

The courts have, however, held that the police do not have to follow these requirements precisely if the circumstances of the case make it appropriate to do otherwise.

Powers to enter premises without a search warrant

Police officers may enter and search premises if it is in order to arrest a person named in an arrest warrant, or to arrest someone for an arrestable offence, or to recapture an escaped prisoner. This power is set out in section 17 of PACE. Reason for the entry must be given to anyone in the premises.

PACE also gives a police officer the right to enter a premises without a search warrant after an arrest if an officer has grounds to believe that there is evidence on the premises relating to the offence for which the person has just been arrested.

To prevent a breach of the peace

There is a right under common law for police to enter premises if there is a need to deal with or prevent a breach of the peace. This right applies even to private homes as was demonstrated by the case of McLeod v Commissioner of Police for the Metropolis (1994) in which the police had entered domestic premises when there was a violent quarrel taking place.

Searching with the consent of the occupier of the premises

The police may enter and search a premises without a warrant if the occupier of these premises gives them permission to do so. This consent must be given in writing and can be withdrawn.

Unlawful entry and search

If a premises is entered and searched unlawfully, where the police exceed their powers a claim for damages can be made under the tort of trespass.

Powers of arrest

Section 24 of PACE sets out the general powers of arrest, and some of these powers can be exercised by private citizens as well as the police.

Arrestable offences

An arrestable offence is:

1. Any offence for which the sentence is fixed by law. An example may be murder which has a fixed term of life imprisonment.
2. Any offence for which the maximum sentence that could be given to an adult is five years imprisonment.
3. Any other offence which Parliament has specifically made an arrestable offence.

PACE Section 24-Arrests by police and private citizens

This section allows the police or a private citizen to arrest without a warrant:

1. Anyone who is in the act of committing an arrestable offence

2. Anyone whom he has reasonable grounds for suspecting to be committing an arrestable offence
3. Anyone who has committed an arrestable offence
4. Where an arrestable offence has been committed, anyone for whom he has reasonable grounds for suspecting to be guilty of it.

The police also have the right to arrest anyone who is about to commit an arrestable offence, anyone whom he has reasonable grounds for suspecting to be about to commit an arrestable offence or where there are reasonable grounds for suspecting that an arrestable offence has been committed.

PACE Section 25

Police have further powers under section 25 to arrest for any offence where the suspects name and address cannot be discovered or that there are reasonable grounds to believe that the name and address given by the suspect are false.

Section 25 also provides powers of arrest where there are reasonable grounds for believing that arrest is necessary to prevent that person from:

- Causing physical injury to himself or others
- Suffering physical injury (i.e. suicide)
- Causing loss or damage to property
- Committing an offence against public decency
- Causing an unlawful obstruction of the highways

Section 25 also gives the police powers to arrest if the arrest is believed to be necessary to protect a child or other vulnerable person.

Other rights of arrest

The Criminal Justice and Public Order Act 1994 added an extra power of arrest to PACE. This is in section 46A of PACE and gives the police the right to arrest without a warrant anyone who has been released on police bail and fails to attend a police station at an allotted time. The Criminal Justice and Public Order Act also gives police the right to arrest for a variety of new offences in connection with collective or aggravated trespass.

Arrest for breach of the peace

The police have a right to arrest where there has been or is likely to be a breach of the peace. The conditions for arrest for breach of the peace were laid down in *Bibby v Chief Constable of Essex Police (2000)*. These are:

- There must be sufficiently real and present threat to the peace
- The threat must come from the person to be arrested
- The conduct of the person must clearly interfere with the rights of others and its natural consequence must be 'not wholly unreasonable' violence from a third party
- The conduct of the person to be arrested must be unreasonable

The right to search an arrested person

Where a person has been arrested the police have a right to search that person for anything which might be used to help an escape or anything that might be evidence relating to an offence.

Powers to detain suspect

Once a person has been arrested and taken to a police station there are rules setting out time limits as to detention. The limits will vary and are longer depending on the severity of the offence. There are also rules, contained in PACE relating to treatment of people in detention.

The general rules are that the police may detain a person for 24 hours. After this the police can detain a person for a further 12 hours but only with the permission of a senior officer. After 36 hours those detained for an ordinary arrestable offence must be released or charged. For serious offences those detained can be held for a further period but a magistrates order must be obtained and the maximum detention cannot exceed 96 hours. There is a right to representation. There is an exception under terrorism offences which allows for detention of 48 hours and up to another 12 days with the Home Secretary's permission.

Rights of detained people
Detainees must be informed of their rights. These include:
- Someone must/can be informed of the arrest

- Being told that independent legal advice is freely available and being allowed to consult with a solicitor
- Being allowed to consult the code of practice

Police interviews

Detained persons may be interviewed by the police. All interviews carried out at a police station must be tape recorded. Suspects have the right to a solicitor during questioning. If a solicitor is not asked for or is late questioning can commence. If the person is under 17 or is mentally handicapped there must be an 'appropriate adult' present during questioning.

Section 76 of PACE states that a court shall not allow statements which have been obtained through oppression to be used as evidence.

The right to silence

A defendant has the right to remain silent but inferences can be drawn from the silence and used in court. The wording of a caution given to a suspect states:
'You do not have to say anything. But it may harm your defence if you do not mentioned when questioned something which you later rely on in court. Anything you do say may be given in evidence'

Searches, fingerprints and samples

When a person is being held at a police station the police do not have an automatic right to search them. However, a custody officer has a duty to record everything a person has with them and if the custody officer thinks a search is necessary then a non-intimate search can be made. A strip search can only take place if it is necessary to remove an article which a person in detention should not be allowed to keep and there is reasonable suspicion that a person may have concealed an article. There are strict rules governing the nature of a strip search and articles of clothing that can be removed at once and in which places.

The police can take fingerprints and non-intimate body samples without the persons consent. Reasonable force can be used to obtain these if necessary. There are different rules for intimate samples. These are defined in the Criminal Justice and Public Order Act 1994 as:

a) a sample of blood, semen or other tissue, fluid, urine or public hair
b) a dental impression
c) a swab taken from a person's body orifice other than the mouth

These can only be taken by a registered medical practitioner or nurse. Samples can be retained.

Complaints against the police

People who believe that the police have acted unjustly and exceeded their powers can complain and the type of complaint will determine how it is dealt with. Minor complaints are dealt with informally and more serious complaints will be dealt with at a higher level.

The independent police complaints commission

This was set up in 2004 to supervise the handling of complaints against the police and associated staff, such as Community Support Officers. The IPCC sets down standards for the police to follow when dealing with complaints. They also monitor the way complaints are dealt with by local police forces.

The IPCC will also investigate serious issues including any accident involving death or serious injury, allegations of corruption, allegations against senior officers, allegations involving racism and allegations of perverting the course of justice.

Any member of the public can complain and complaints can be made directly to the IPCC or through organisations such as the Citizens Advice Bureau or through the Council for Racial Equality or the Youth Offending Team. It is also possible to complain through a solicitor or an MP. Where the police have committed a crime in the execution of their duties criminal action can be brought against them.

9

Hearing Criminal Cases

As the criminal law is set down by the state, bringing a prosecution for breach of criminal law is seen as the role of the state. The majority of prosecutions are brought by the Crown Prosecution Service which is the agency of the state for criminal prosecutions.

A criminal prosecution can also be brought by an individual or company although this is rare. The following is an outline of the procedure for criminal trials.

Pre-trial hearings

All criminal cases will first go to the magistrates court and, in most cases, will be referred to a higher court unless the offence is minor or the person(s) plead guilty.

Categories of criminal offences

Criminal offences are divided into three main categories as follows:

1. Summary offences. These are the least serious and are always tried in the Magistrates Court. They include nearly all driving offences, common assault and criminal damage of less than £5,000.

2. Triable either way offences. These are a middle range type offence and can include assault causing actual bodily harm. These cases can be tried either in the Magistrates Court or the Crown Court.

3. Indictable offences. These are more serious crimes such as rape or murder. All such offences must be tried at the Crown Court, the first hearing being at the Magistrates Court.

Bail

One matter to be decided pre-trial is that of bail, whether the defendant should stay in custody while awaiting trial or whether he or she should be released on bail. Being granted bail means that the person is at liberty until the next stage of the case.

The police may release a suspect on bail while they pursue their enquiries. The suspect must return to the police station at a specified date in the future. The police can also grant bail to a defendant who has been charged with an offence. In this case the person is bailed to appear at a Magistrates Court at a later date. The decision on whether to grant bail or not is made by a custody officer under section 38 of PACE. Bail can be refused if the suspects name and address cannot be ascertained or there is doubt as to the validity of information.

The principles as to when bail should be granted are contained within the Bail Act 1976. This is the key Act, starting with the assumption that an accused person should be granted bail, though this right can be limited for certain cases such as terrorism or repeat serious offences. Section 4 of the Bail Act 1976 gives a general right to bail, but this can be withdrawn if the court believes that there are grounds for believing the defendant, if released, would fail to surrender to custody, commit an offence whilst on bail or interfere with witnesses or obstruct the course of justice.

In deciding whether to grant bail the court will consider various factors:

- The nature and seriousness of the offence
- The character of the defendant and community ties
- The record of the defendant
- The strength of evidence against the defendant.

The courts have the powers to impose conditions on the granting of bail. These are similar to those granted to the police, as outlined below.

Bail sureties

The courts or police can require a surety for bail. This is another person who is willing to pay a sum of money if that person doesn't turn up to court. No money is paid until the defendant breaks bail.

If any person granted bail by the police fails to attend the next stage of the case then the police can make an arrest.

Like the courts, the police have powers to impose conditions on bail. These are contained within the Criminal Justice and Public Order Act 1994. These conditions can vary, ranging from surrender of passport to regular reporting at a police station.

If the police are not prepared to grant bail then they must bring the suspect before a magistrates court. The magistrates can then make a decision as to whether the suspect should be released on bail.

Restrictions on bail do exist, such as terrorism cases and situations where there have been repeated serious offences.

Section 19 of the Criminal Justice Act 2003 amended the Bail Act 1976 and placed certain restrictions on bail for adult drug offenders who have tested positive for specific Class A drugs where the offender is either charged with possession or possession with intent to supply a Class A drug or the court is satisfied that there are grounds for believing that misuse of a class A drug contributed to the offence or that the offence was motivated wholly or partly by the intended misuse of a drug and the defendant has refused to participate in an assessment or follow up in relation to the dependency on Class A drugs.

The prosecution in a case can appeal against the granting of bail. This is set out in the Bail (Amendment) Act 1993.

The Crown Prosecution Service

The Crown Prosecution Service (CPS) was established by the Prosecution of Offences Act 1985 and began life in 1986. The head of the CPS is the Director of Public

Prosecutions who must have been a qualified lawyer for 10 years. The DPP is appointed by the Attorney General. Under the DPP are Chief Crown Prosecutors who each head one of 42 areas. Each area is sub-divided into branches, each of which is headed by a Branch Crown prosecutor. Within branches there are lawyers and support staff who are given responsibility for cases.

The functions of the CPS involve all aspects of prosecution as outlined below:

- Deciding on what offences should be charged
- Reviewing all cases given to them by the police to see if there is sufficient evidence to proceed and whether it is in the public interest to do so
- Taking responsibility for the case
- Conducting the prosecution of cases in the Magistrates Court
- Conducting cases in the Crown Court

Once a defendant has been charged with an offence then the police role in the matter is over and the case is handed over to the CPS.

Criminal courts

The two courts which hear criminal cases are the Magistrates Court and the Crown Court. If a defendant in either one of these courts pleads guilty to a charge against them the role of the court is to pass sentence. Where the accused pleads not guilty the role of the court is to try the case and establish whether the defendant is guilty or not guilty. The burden of proof is on the prosecution who must prove the case beyond reasonable doubt. The form of trial is adversarial with prosecution and defence presenting their cases and cross-examining witnesses while the role of the judge is to be a referee, overseeing the trial and ensuring that the law is adhered to. The judge does not investigate the case.

The role of the Magistrates Court

There are about 430 Magistrates Courts in England and Wales. Magistrates Courts are local courts and they will be in almost every town whilst big cities will usually have several. Cases are heard by magistrates, who may be either qualified District Judges or unqualified lay justices. There is a legally qualified clerk attached to each court to provide assistance.

Magistrates Courts have jurisdiction in a variety of matters. They will:

- Try all summary cases
- Try any triable either way offences which it has been decided should be dealt with in the Magistrates Court
- Deal with the first hearings of all indictable offences
- Deal with other matters connected to criminal offences such as issuing warrants for bail and deciding bail applications
- Try cases in the Youth Court where the defendant is aged 10-17

The Magistrates Courts also have some civil jurisdiction including enforcing council tax demands and issuing warrants of entry and investigation to utilities such as gas and electricity, family cases, proceedings concerning the welfare of children under the Children Act 1989.

Summary Trials

Summary trials are the least serious criminal offences. They are further divided into offences on different levels ranging from level one (lowest) to level five (highest). Fines are set in accordance with each level. For level one the fine is maximum £200, level two £500, level three £1,000, level four £2,500 and level five £5,000. These fines arise from the Criminal Justice Act 1991 and are increased periodically to account for inflation. The maximum prison sentence that can be given for summary offences is six months which will shortly be increased to 15 months following the passing of the Criminal Justice Act 2003.

At the start of any summary trial the defendant will be asked whether he or she pleads guilty or not guilty. If a guilty plea is entered the case will be explained to the court and the prosecutor and defence will put their case and the magistrates will decide sentence.

If a not guilty plea is entered, the procedure is rather more complicated as the prosecutor has to provide evidence to the court and prove the case. Witnesses are called. At the end the defence can call for the case to be dismissed on lack of evidence if this is the case. The magistrates will then decide on the case, whether guilty or not guilty.

Triable either way cases

Plea before venue

Under this procedure the defendant is asked whether he pleads guilty. If the plea is guilty then there is no right to ask to go to a Crown Court although the magistrate may still decide to send him there for sentence.

If the defendant pleads not guilty then the magistrates must carry out 'mode of trial' proceedings to establish where the case will be tried. Under section 19 of the Magistrates Court Act 1980 they must consider the nature and seriousness of the case and decide a course of action. If the case involves complex cases of law it will usually be referred to the Crown Court. It will also be referred to the Crown Court if it is of a particularly serious nature and has, for example, involved organised crime or where the amount involved was particularly high, more than twice the potential fine that magistrates can levy.

In cases, rare cases, where the Attorney General, Solicitor General or Director of Public Prosecutions is the prosecutor, magistrates must abide by the wishes of the prosecutor and send the case to the Crown Court if this is what is wanted.

If magistrates accept jurisdiction, the defendant is informed that he has the right to trial by jury, in the

Crown Court, but may be tried by magistrates if he so wishes. If the magistrates feel that they have insufficient powers to punish they can refer the matter to the Crown Court for sentencing.

Sending cases to the Crown Court

For indictable offences the case is automatically referred by magistrates to the Crown Court. Section 51 of the Crime and Disorder Act 1988 dictates this. For triable either way offences, magistrates will hold a plea before venue and, if the plea is not guilty, a mode of trial hearing. The decision to try the case in the Magistrates Court or the Crown Court is taken at this point.

Committal proceedings

Magistrates can commit a defendant charged with a triable either way offence for sentence in the Crown Court.

Role of the court clerk

Every bench of magistrates is assisted by a clerk who is also a legal advisor. The senior clerk in each court has to be a barrister or solicitor of at least five years standing. The role of the clerk is to guide the magistrates on questions of law, practice and procedure.

Youth courts

Youth offenders aged between 10-17 are dealt with in the Youth court which is a branch of the Magistrates court. Children under the age of 10 cannot be charged with a criminal offence. There are some exceptional cases where the case can be tried in the Crown Court if the charge is one of manslaughter or murder, rape or causing death by dangerous driving. In addition, it is possible to send a person over 14 to the Crown Court if the charge is sufficiently serious.

Appeals from the Magistrates Court

The system of appeal routes from the magistrate's court will depend on whether the appeal is on a point of law or for other reasons. The two appeal routes are the Crown Court or the Queens Bench Divisional Court.

The normal route of appeal is the Crown Court and can only be used by the defence. If the defendant has pleaded guilty then the appeal can only be against sentence. If the plea was not guilty then the appeal can be against conviction or sentence. In both cases the defendant has the automatic right to appeal.

Further appeal to the House of Lords

From the decision of the Queens Bench Court there is a possibility of a further appeal to the House of Lords. This can only be made if:

1. The Divisional Court certifies that a point of law of general public importance is involved.
2. The Divisional Court or the House of Lords gives leave to appeal because the point is one which ought to be considered by the House of Lords.

The Crown Court

The Courts Act 1971 set up the Crown Court to deal with all cases that were not tried at the Magistrates Court. The Crown Court sits in 90 different centres throughout England and Wales. There are three kinds of centre:

1. First tier-these exist in main centres throughout the country. At each court there is a High court and a Crown Court. The Crown Court is staffed by High Court Judges as well as Circuit Judges and Recorders. The court can deal with all categories of crime triable on indictment.
2. Second tier-this is a Crown Court only, but High Court judges can sit there on a regular basis to hear cases, as well as Circuit Judges and Recorders.
3. Third tier-this is staffed by Circuit judges and Recorders. The most serious cases are not usually tried here.

Preliminary matters in the Crown Court

The indictment

The indictment is a document which formally sets out charges against a defendant.

Disclosure by prosecution and defence

The Criminal Procedure and Investigations Act 1996 places a duty on both sides to make certain points of the case known to each other. The 1996 Act also imposes a duty on the defence in cases which are to be tried on indictment. After the prosecutors initial disclosure, the defence must give a written statement to the prosecution setting out:

1. the nature of the accused persons defence
2. the matters on which he takes issue with the prosecution and why he intends to take issue
3. any point of law which he wishes to take, and the case authority on which he will rely.
4.

Details of alibis and witnesses he intends to call to support the alibi. This information gives the prosecution time to carry out police checks on the witnesses.

A preliminary hearing called a 'plea and directions' hearing is held after a case has been forwarded to a Crown Court, normally within four weeks if the defendant is being held in custody and six weeks if not. The purpose of this hearing is to discover whether the plea is guilty or not guilty. All charges are read out in open court and the defendant will plead one way or the other. This is called the 'arraignment'. If the defendant pleads guilty the judge will sentence the defendant immediately, if possible. Where a defendant pleads not guilty the judge will require the defence and prosecution to identify the key issues of fact and law that are involved in the case. He will then give directions that are necessary for the organisation of the trial.

The trial
A defendant appearing at the Crown Court will usually be represented by a barrister and sometimes a solicitor.

Under s36 of the Criminal Justice Act 1988 the Attorney general can apply for leave to refer what is considered to be an unduly lenient sentence to the Court of Appeal for re-sentencing.

Appeals to the House of Lords

Both prosecution and defence may appeal from the Court of Appeal to the House of Lords. However, it is necessary to get the case certified as involving a point of law of general public importance, either from the Court of appeal or the House of Lords.

References to the European Court of Justice

In a case where a point of European law is involved it is possible for any court to make reference to the European Court of Justice under Article 177 of the Treaty of Rome.

Sentencing

Judges and magistrates have a fairly wide discretion when it comes to passing sentence on a guilty party, although they are subject to certain restrictions. Magistrates can only impose a maximum of six months imprisonment for one offence and twelve months for two. The Criminal Justice Act 2003 provides powers to increase the sentence for one offence to 12 months and two or more offences 15 months.

Judges in the Crown Court can impose up to life imprisonment for some crimes and there is no maximum figure for fines.

There are certain other restrictions placed on the Magistrates and Crown Courts by Parliament. The maximum sentence to be handed out varies depending on the crime and Parliament determines the length of sentences.

Murder carries a mandatory life sentence, whereas the judge can work within the parameters of maximum of life for other crimes such as rape and manslaughter.

When judges or magistrates pass sentence they will look at what they are trying to achieve when sentencing. Section 142 of the Criminal Justice Act 2003 sets out the purpose of sentencing for those aged 18 and over. This states that the court must have regard to:

- the punishment of offenders
- the reduction of crime
- the reform and rehabilitation of offenders
- the protection of the public
- the making of reparation by offenders to persons affected by their offences

Courts have several different types of sentences available to them. There are four main categories: custodial sentences, community sentences, fines and discharges.

Custodial sentences

This is imprisonment and is the most serious sentence that a court can pass. Prison can range from a weekend to life. Custodial sentences include:

- mandatory and discretionary life sentences
- fixed term sentences
- short term sentences
- intermittent custody
- suspended sentences

Community sentences

Prior to the Criminal Justice Act 2003, the courts had individual community sentences that they could impose on an offender. The Act created one community order under which the courts can combine any requirements that they think are necessary. These requirements include all the previous existing community sentences which become available as 'requirements' or sentences required to rehabilitate the offender, and can be attached to the sentence. The sentence is available for offenders of 16 or over. The full list of 'requirements' is set out in s 177 of the Criminal Justice Act 2003 which states:

'177 (1) Where a person aged 16 or over is convicted of an offence, the court by or before which he is convicted may make an order imposing on him any one or more of the following requirements:

   a) an unpaid work requirement
   b) an activity requirement
   c) a programme requirement
   d) a prohibited activity requirement
   e) a curfew requirement
   f) an exclusion requirement
   g) a residence requirement
   h) a mental health treatment requirement

i) a drug rehabilitation requirement
j) an alcohol treatment requirement
k) a supervision requirement
l) in the case where an offender is under 25, an attendance centre requirement.

Fines

The maximum fine in a Magistrates court is £5,000. The magistrates can impose a fine of up to £20,000 on businesses which have committed offences under various regulatory legislation such as health and safety at work.

Discharges

A discharge can be conditional or absolute. Conditional discharge means that the discharge is on condition that no further offence is committed in a set period up to three years. An absolute discharge means that no penalty has been imposed.

Other powers available to the courts

Courts can order compensation to a victim of crime. In the Magistrates court the maximum compensation is £5,000. If the defendant still has the property that he took from the victim then the court can order that it be returned. This is called a restitution order.

A court can order that a person be deprived of property that he has used to commit the offence. There is special power to order forfeiture in drug related cases. The

Proceeds of Crime Act 1995 also gives the courts powers to take from criminals all profits from crime for up to six years before conviction.

Young offenders

As with adult offenders the courts have powers to order custodial sentences, fines and discharges but there are a range of different sentences available and also restrictions on what the courts can order. As far as community sentences are concerned, young offenders aged 16 or over can be given the same sentences as adults. They cannot be used for offenders under the age of 16. However, Curfew Orders can be used for those over 10 years of age. There are a number of other orders aimed at young offenders:

Attendance centre orders

This type of order is only for those under 25 and is available for all young offenders from 10 years onwards. It involves attendance at a special centre for two or three hours a week up to a maximum of 36 hours for 16-24 year olds and 24 hours for 10-15 year olds. The minimum number of hours is usually 12 but can be less for offenders under 14. The centres are run by the probation services and are usually on a Saturday afternoons. An attendance centre order cannot be made if an offender has served a period of detention previously.

Supervision orders
Section 69 of the Crime and Disorder Act 1998 created a new community order called an Action Plan order. The

courts can impose this on offenders under the age of 18. The order places the offender under supervision and also sets out requirements the offender has to comply with in respect to his actions and whereabouts during a period of three months. The requirements can be any one of the following:

- To participate in set activities
- To present himself to a specified person at set times and places
- To attend at an attendance centre
- To stay away from certain places
- To comply with arrangements for his education
- To make reparation

Fines for young offenders

The maximum amount of the fine varies with the age of the offender. 10-13 year olds can only be fined a maximum of £250, 14-17 year olds £1,000. Those over 18 are subject to adult rules.

Reparation orders

A Reparation Order may be imposed on offenders under the age of 18. This order cannot be made in combination with a custodial sentence. Community Service Order, a combination order, a supervision order or an Action Plan Order.

An order will require the defendant to make reparation as defined in the order:

- To a person or persons who were victims of the offence or were otherwise affected by it, or
- To the community at large

The order is for a maximum of 24 hours work and the order must be completed under supervision within three months of its imposition. An order for direct reparation to a person can only be made with that persons consent.

Discharges

These may be used for an offender of any age and are most commonly used for young first time offenders who have committed minor crimes. The courts cannot conditionally discharge an offender where a child or young offender has been warned within the previous two years, unless there are exceptional circumstances. Also, the courts cannot conditionally discharge an offender where the offender is in breach of an anti-social behaviour order or where the offender is in breach of a sex offender order.

Reprimands and warnings

These are methods with which the police can deal with young offenders without bringing them to court. There is a limit to the number of times and occasions that an offender can be cautioned.

Responsibility of parents

Parents can be bound over to keep their child under control for a set period of time up to one year. The parents must agree to this. If the child then commits an offence within this period the parents must pay a sum up to £1,000 maximum.

Where an offender under 16 is fined or ordered to pay compensation, the court must order the parents to pay. The financial situation of the parents is taken into account when assessing the amount.

Parenting orders

Parenting orders are intended to offer training and support to parents to help change their children's offending behaviour. Under a parenting order a parent can be required to attend counselling or guidance sessions for up to three months on a basis of a maximum once per week.

In addition, the parent may be required to comply with conditions imposed by the court. A court may make a parenting order where:

- The court makes a Child safety Order
- The court makes an anti-social behaviour order or sex offender order in respect of the child
- A child or young person is convicted of an offence
- A parent is convicted of an offence related to truancy under the Education Act 1996.

Offenders who are mentally ill

The law recognises, as far as it possibly can, that mentally ill offenders should receive treatment as opposed to punishment. Courts have a wide range of powers available to them when dealing with such offenders. The main extra powers available to courts are to give the offender a community sentence with a requirement that he or she attends for treatment, make a hospital order or to make a restriction order under the Mental Health Act 1983 section 41.

Under the same section, offenders with severe mental health problems can be sent to high security hospitals such as Broadmoor. Such an order can only be made by the Crown Court.

Anti-social behaviour orders

Known as ASBO's these are civil orders. They are imposed on a person who has behaved in an anti-social way. The type of behaviour termed anti-social is very wide and can include drunkenness, drug taking or causing prolonged and excessive nuisance to neighbours or the wider community.

Under an ASBO a person can be ordered not to repeat a certain anti-social behaviour or not to go to a certain place. In short it has the effect of an injunction.

10

Juries

Juries have been in the legal system for a long time, over one thousand years. Only a small percentage of cases is tried by jury today. However, juries are used in the following courts:

- Crown Court for criminal trials on indictment
- High Court (Queens Bench Division (only for certain cases)
- County Court for similar cases to the Queens Bench Division
- Coroners Courts

The most important use of juries is in the Crown Court in criminal trials, where they decide the guilt or otherwise of the defendant. However, given that most criminal cases are decided in the Magistrates Court only about 1% of all criminal cases are tried in the Crown Court by jury.

Civil cases

Juries in civil cases are used in only limited circumstances. The present rules for when juries may be tried in civil cases are set out in section 69 of the Supreme Court Act 1981 for High Court cases, and section 66 of the County Courts Act 1984 for cases in the

County Court. The Acts state that parties have the right to jury trial only in the following types of case:

- Defamation
- False imprisonment
- Malicious prosecution
- Fraud

The present qualifications to be a juror are set out in the Juries Act 1974 (as amended). To qualify for jury service a person must be:

- Aged between 18-70
- Registered as a voter
- Resident in the United Kingdom, the Channel Islands or the Isle of man for at least five years since their thirteenth birthday and must not be:
- A mentally disordered person or disqualified from jury service

Disqualification from jury service involves having a criminal record, usually one that has entailed serving a term in prison, a suspended sentence or a community sentence. In addition, anyone who is currently on bail in criminal proceedings is disqualified from sitting as a juror.

Selecting a jury

At each Crown Court there is an official who is responsible for summonsing enough jurors to try the cases to be heard in each two-week period. The official will arrange for names to be selected at random from the electoral registers for the area which the court covers. Those summonsed must notify the court of for any reason they cannot attend. All others are expected to attend for two weeks jury service. If a trial carries on for longer than two weeks then the jury will be expected to stay on longer.

Routine police checks are carried out on prospective jurors to eliminate those with unsuitable criminal backgrounds. A further check is made on a juror's background to ascertain political affiliations although this should be carried out only in exceptional circumstances and can only be carried out with the Attorney General's permission.

Juries are usually divided into groups of 15 and 12 will be selected to hear a case. Once they have been selected these jurors come into the jury box to be sworn in as jurors. At this point, before the jury has been sworn in, both the prosecution and defence have certain rights to challenge one or more of the jurors. There are two challenges that can be made and, in addition, the prosecution have a special right of 'stand by'. These are:

- to the array
- for cause
- prosecution right to stand by jurors

To the array-this right to challenge arises from the Juries Act 1974 and it is a challenge to the whole jury on the basis that it has been chosen in an unrepresentative or biased way.

For causes-this involves challenging the right of an individual juror to sit on a jury.

Prosecution right to stand by jurors-this is a right that only the prosecution can exercise. It allows the juror who has been stood by to be put at the end of the list of potential jurors so that they will not be used unless there is a lack of jurors.

Juries role in criminal cases

The jury is only used at the Crown Court where the defendant pleads not guilty. The trial is presided over by a judge and the functions split between judge and jury. The judge will decide points of law and the jury decides the facts. At the end of a case, the judge can direct a jury to acquit a defendant if he feels that the prosecutions evidence does not make a case. This is called a directed acquittal.

Majority verdicts

If, after at least two hours (longer where there are several defendants) the jury have not reached a verdict the judge can call them back into the courtroom and direct them to pass a majority verdict. Where there is a full jury of 12, the verdict can be 10-2 or 11-1 either for guilty or not guilty. If the jury has fallen below 12 for any reason then only one can disagree with the verdict. A jury cannot go below nine.

The jury discussion takes place in secret and there can be no enquiry as to how the jury reached its verdict. Section

8 of the Contempt of Court Act 1981 makes disclosure of anything that happens in a jury room a contempt of court which is a criminal act.

11

Legal aid and advice

Many people will require legal assistance of one sort or another when either taking or defending a legal action. Lack of knowledge and difficulty in meeting costs are the two main reasons for needing assistance.

The Access to Justice Act 1999 replaced the old legal aid schemes with the Community Legal service for civil matters and the Criminal defence Service for criminal cases. To oversee the public funding of legal services there is a Legal Services Commission.

The Legal Services Commission

Section 1 of the Access to Justice Act 1999 set up this Commission. The members are appointed by the Lord Chancellor. The Legal Services Commission took over funding of civil cases from the Legal Aid Board. It is responsible for managing the Community Legal Service Fund and is responsible for developing plans locally and nationally for legal funding.

The Community Legal Service

The CLS provides the following services for matters involving civil law:

- General information about the law and legal system and availability of legal services
- Help in preventing or settling or otherwise resolving disputes about legal rights and duties
- Help in enforcing decisions by which such disputes are resolved
- Help in relation to legal proceedings not related to disputes

This scheme includes advice, assistance and representation by lawyers as well as the services of non-lawyers. It also covers mediation. The money to fund this comes from the Community Legal Services fund.

The Community Legal Services Fund

This will fund a range of different types of legal services. The Legal Services Commission maintains the fund and money is allocated annually by the Lord Chancellor. Certain types of civil matters cannot be met out of the fund. These are:

- Allegations of injury caused by negligence, death or damage to property, apart from allegations of criminal negligence
- Conveyancing
- Boundary disputes
- The making of wills
- Matters of trust law
- Defamation or malicious falsehood
- Matters of company or partnership law

- Other matters arising out of the carrying on of a business

Court cases

Funding is available for cases in the County Court, High Court and Appeal Court. Cases for amounts under £5,000 cannot get funding.

Different types of help

The person making the application must demonstrate, by a means test, that they are eligible for help. Once a person is eligible there are a number of levels of help. For civil cases, these are:

- Legal help-this covers advice but not issuing or conducting court proceedings
- Help at court-this allows help at court or tribunal although without formally acting as representative
- Legal representation-this covers all aspects of a case including starting or defending court proceedings and any advocacy needed in a case
- Support funding-this allows partial funding of cases which are otherwise being pursued privately

In addition, there are two other levels available in family cases. The main one is Approved Family Help which provides advice and negotiation, issuing of proceedings and any conveyancing work deemed necessary. The other service is Family Mediation which covers the cost of mediation to resolve a family dispute.

Funding criteria

As stated, applicants for legal funding have to undergo a means test to determine whether they are eligible for aid. Two matters are taken into consideration, disposable income and disposable capital.

Disposable income

Disposable income is calculated by starting with gross income and deducting:

- Tax and national insurance
- Housing Costs
- Childcare costs or maintenance paid for children
- An allowance for each dependant
- A standard allowance for employment (where applicant is employed)

Those in receipt of income support or income based job seekers allowance will qualify automatically assuming that their disposable capital is within the set limit.

Disposable capital

Disposable capital is the assets of the person, such as money in the bank or stocks and shares. For Legal Help, Help at Court and representation in Immigration cases the limit for disposable capital is £3,000. Funding is not available for those with capital over this amount.

For the other publicly funded services there is a minimum limit for disposable capital of £3,000 and a maximum of £8,000. Within that band the contribution will vary according to the amount of disposable capital.

Criteria for funding

There is a code about provision of funded services. The factors which are considered are as follows:

- The likely cost of funding and the benefit which may be obtained
- The availability of money in the Community legal Fund
- The importance of matters for the individual
- The availability of other services
- The prospects of success
- The conduct of the individual
- The public interest
- Any other matters which the Lord Chancellor may require the Commission to consider

Providers of services

Legal services are provided by a broad range of people and organisations. Local solicitors are a main provider but there are other agencies such as advice agencies and consumer protection groups who can provide advice.

The Legal Services Commission grants contracts to service providers. There are currently about 5,000 firms of solicitors with contracts and they have to meet stringent criteria based on quality of advice given.

Conditional fees

Conditional fee cases were developed as a result of the problem arising because of the unknown costs of court action putting off many people from taking legal action. The solicitor and a client will agree on a fee which would normally be involved in a case. The agreement will also stipulate the solicitors 'success fee'. If the solicitor does not win the case then no fee is charged. If the case is won then the normal fee plus the success fee is paid. Most solicitors will include a cap on the success fee, which means that it cannot be more than 25% of damages awarded.

Law centres

Law centres offer a free non-means tested legal service to people in their area. Funding has always been a problem for law centres and many are reliant on grants. As a result many have closed. Those which have remained open will deal with the needs of the community they serve, undertaking work such as housing, planning, the environment, employment, immigration and consumer matters. The list is not exhaustive.

The Criminal Defence Service

Under s 12 of the Access to Justice act 1999, The Legal services Commission established a Legal Defence Service. This service is aimed at ' securing that individuals involved in criminal investigations or proceedings have access to such advice, assistance or representation as the interests of justice require'. The following schemes are offered:

Duty Solicitors

Section 13 of the Access to Justice Act 1999 states that the Commission shall fund advice and assistance as it considers appropriate for individuals who are arrested and held in custody. However, solicitors can no longer attend at a police station, unless the client is vulnerable, where the client is detained for:

- a non-imprisonable offence
- on a warrant
- in breach of bail conditions
- for drink drive offences.

Advice and assistance

This is limited to several hours work and can only include advocacy if the solicitor has applied for a representation order which has been refused. Usually, there is a means test for advice and assistance. However, a duty solicitor at a magistrates court can see all defendants in custody free of charge under the advice and assistance scheme.

Representation

This covers the costs of a solicitor to prepare the defence before the case gets to court. It also covers representation at court, including issues such as bail. If a barrister is required then this will be covered. There will be a merits case for representation and the judge can also order the defendant to pay some of the costs at the end of the trial.